PIANO • VOCAL • GUITAR

Award-Winning Songs

of the
Country Music Association

**VOLUME 3
(1997-2000)**

ISBN 0-634-03531-2

HAL•LEONARD®
CORPORATION
7777 W. BLUEMOUND RD. P.O. BOX 13819 MILWAUKEE, WI 53213

Visit Hal Leonard Online at
www.halleonard.com

CMA Awards
Country Music's Biggest Night

Through the Country Music Association's leadership and guidance, Country Music has become one of America's most diplomatic ambassadors to the world. Industry leaders readily admit that CMA has won global recognition and has been the most important force in the worldwide growth and expansion of Country Music. The first trade organization ever formed to promote a type of music, CMA, founded in 1958, originally consisted of only 233 members and now boasts more than 7,000 members in 40 countries.

One of CMA's most significant achievements is the CMA Awards which has been on national television each year since 1968. Considered the Country Music industry's most highly-coveted and pre-eminent awards, the accolades are presented annually to outstanding Country artists, songwriters, producers, video directors, publishers, radio personalities and radio programmers, as voted by CMA's membership, to honor excellence in artistry. Membership in CMA is open to those persons or organizations presently or formerly active, directly or indirectly, in the field of Country Music.

Any Country Music song with original words and music is eligible for the CMA Song of the Year nomination, based upon the song's Country singles chart activity during the eligibility period, which spans from July 1 through June 30 of each year. Nominations from the CMA membership, in addition to the top five songs from the combined tabulation of the Country singles charts from BILLBOARD, the GAVIN REPORT, and RADIO & RECORDS, are voted on through balloting by the entire CMA membership. From this, the top five songs appear on the final ballot with Song of the Year being selected and first announced on the CMA Awards telecast.

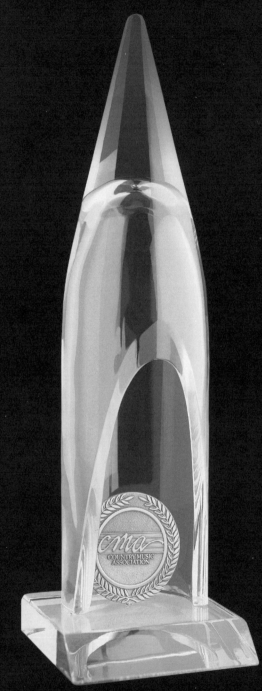

CMA AWARD *Vital Statistics*

Height: 14.25 inches

Weight: 5.24 pounds

Material: Handblown Italian crystal obelisk
            and base with beveled edge.

CMA three level die-struck medallion with
polished bronze finish.

Nameplates are 1 inch x 3 inches satin brass
with beveled edges.

Award-Winning Songs

of the
Country Music Association

Nominees and Winners of the CMA Song of the Year

	Song	Recorded by
11	All the Good Ones Are Gone	*Pam Tillis*
16	Amazed	*Lonestar*
26	Blue	*LeAnn Rimes*
30	Breathe	*Faith Hill*
21	A Broken Wing	*Martina McBride*
36	Butterfly Kisses	*Bob Carlisle*
42	Don't Laugh at Me	*Mark Wills*
47	He Didn't Have to Be	*Brad Paisley*
54	Holes in the Floor of Heaven* *(1998)*	*Steve Wariner*
64	How Do I Live	*Trisha Yearwood*
59	Husbands and Wives	*Brooks & Dunn*
68	I Hope You Dance* *(2000)*	*Lee Ann Womack with Sons of the Desert*
76	I Just Want to Dance with You	*George Strait*
81	If You Ever Have Forever in Mind	*Vince Gill*
86	It's Your Love	*Tim McGraw with Faith Hill*
92	Murder on Music Row	*George Strait*
104	Please Remember Me	*Tim McGraw*
99	Strawberry Wine* *(1997)*	*Deana Carter*
112	This Kiss* *(1999)*	*Faith Hill*
116	Time Marches On	*Tracy Lawrence*

*CMA Song of the Year

PAM TILLIS
"All the Good Ones Are Gone"

LONESTAR
"Amazed"

LEANN RIMES
"Blue"

FAITH HILL
"Breathe"
"It's Your Love" (with Tim McGraw)
"This Kiss"

MARTINA McBRIDE
"A Broken Wing"

BRAD PAISLEY
"He Didn't Have to Be"

STEVE WARINER
"Holes in the Floor of Heaven"

TRISHA YEARWOOD
"How Do I Live"

BROOKS & DUNN
"Husbands and Wives"

LEE ANN WOMACK
"I Hope You Dance"
(with Sons of the Desert)

GEORGE STRAIT
"I Just Want to Dance with You"
"Murder on Music Row"

VINCE GILL
"If You Ever Have Forever in Mind"

TIM McGRAW
"It's Your Love" (with Faith Hill)
"Please Remember Me"

MARK WILLS
"Don't Laugh at Me"

DEANA CARTER
"Strawberry Wine"

TRACY LAWRENCE
"Time Marches On"

ALL THE GOOD ONES ARE GONE

Words and Music by DEAN DILLON
and BOB McDILL

AMAZED

Words and Music by MARV GREEN,
CHRIS LINDSEY and AIMEE MAYO

Moderately slow Country Ballad

*Recorded a half step lower.

A BROKEN WING

Words and Music by SAM HOGIN,
PHIL BARNHART and JAMES HOUSE

She loved him like he was ___ the last man on earth.

Gave him ev-'ry-thing she ev-er had.

Original key: B major. This edition has been transposed up one half-step to be more playable.

With a _____ bro - ken wing, _____ she _____ car - ries her dreams.

Man, you ought to see her fly.

BLUE

Words and Music by
BILL MACK

BREATHE

Words and Music by HOLLY LAMAR
and STEPHANIE BENTLEY

Moderately fast

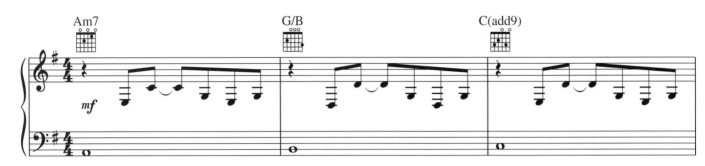

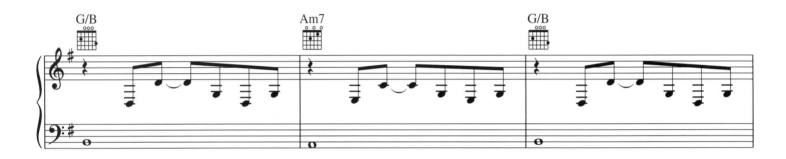

I can feel the mag - ic float - ing in

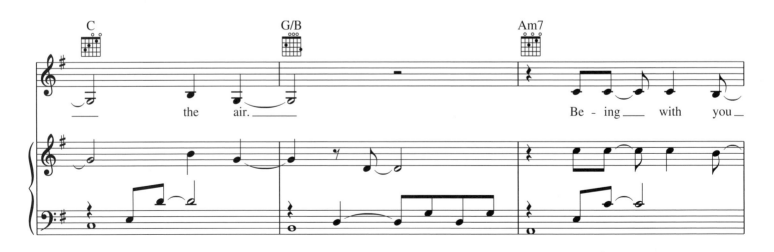

the air. ___ Be - ing ___ with you ___

BUTTERFLY KISSES

Words and Music by BOB CARLISLE
and RANDY THOMAS

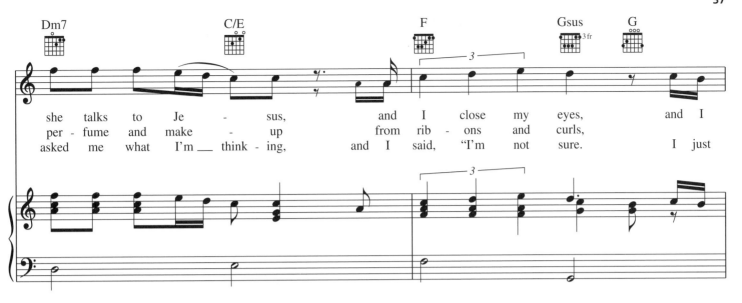

she talks to Je - sus,   and I close my eyes,   and I
per - fume and make - up   from rib - ons and curls,
asked me what I'm ___ think - ing,   and I said, "I'm not sure.   I just

thank God ___ for all ___   of the joy in my ___ life.
try - ing ___ her wings out   in a great big world. _____
feel like ___ I'm los - ing   my ba - by girl." ___

Oh, but most of all,   for but - ter - fly kiss - es ___   af - ter
But I re - mem - ber   but - ter - fly kiss - es ___   af - ter
Then she leaned o - ver, gave me but - ter - fly kiss - es ___   with her

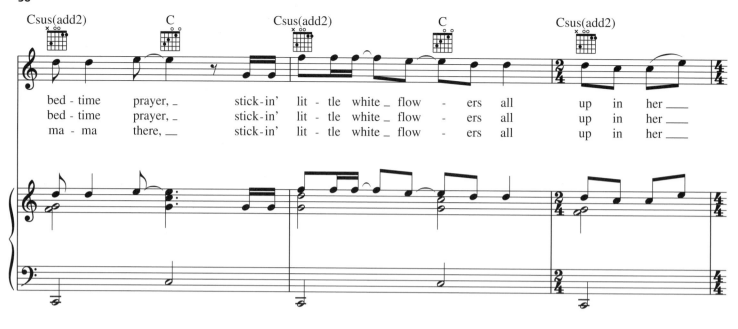

bed - time   prayer, __   stick-in' lit - tle white _ flow - ers all   up in her ___
bed - time   prayer, __   stick-in' lit - tle white _ flow - ers all   up in her ___
ma - ma   there, __   stick-in' lit - tle white _ flow - ers all   up in her ___

hair.   "Walk be - side ___ the po - ny, dad - dy, it's
hair.   "You know how much __ I love __ you, dad - dy, but if
hair.   "Walk me down __ the aisle, __ dad - dy, it's

my first   ride. ___   I know the cake __ looks fun - ny, dad - dy, but
you don't   mind, ___   I'm on - ly goin' __ to kiss __ you on ___ the
just a - bout time.   Does my wed - ding gown __ look pret - ty, dad - dy? Dad -

DON'T LAUGH AT ME

Words and Music by STEVE SESKIN
and ALLEN SHAMBLIN

lit-tle boy with glass-es, the one they call a geek. _ A lit-tle
crip-ple on the cor-ner, you pass me on the street. _ I ____

girl who nev-er smiles _ 'cause I've got brac-es on _ my teeth. And
would-n't be out here beg-gin' if I had e-nough_ to eat. And

HE DIDN'T HAVE TO BE

Words and Music by KELLEY LOVELACE
and BRAD PAISLEY

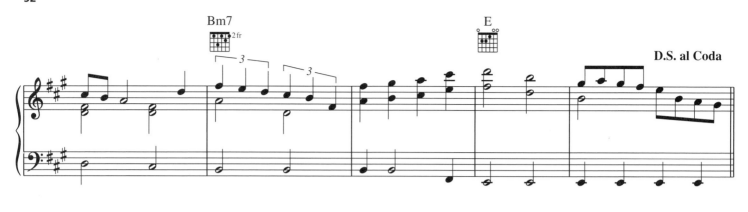

D.S. al Coda

CODA

Yeah, I hope I'm at least ____

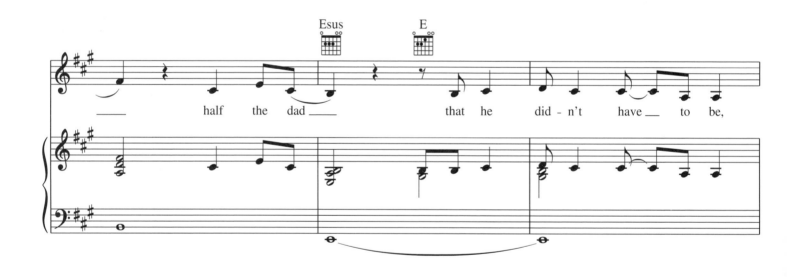

____ half the dad ____ that he did-n't have ____ to be,

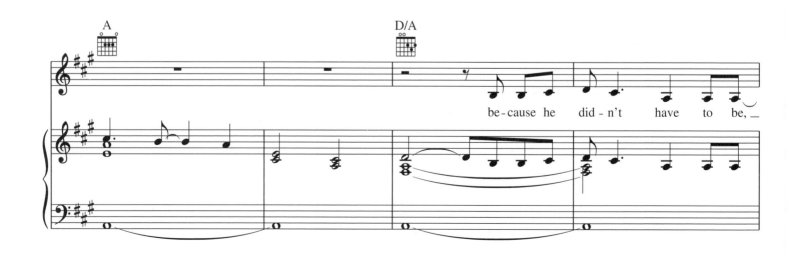

be-cause he did-n't have to be, ____

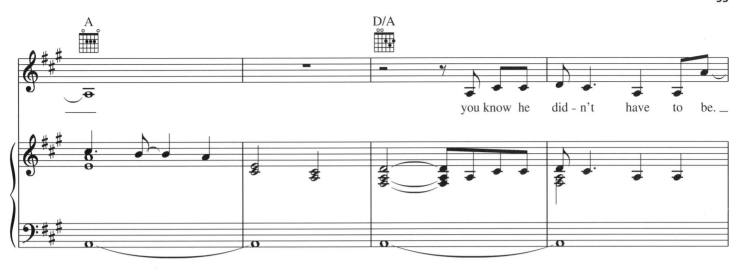

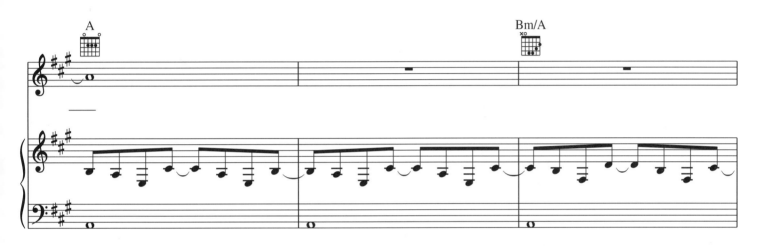

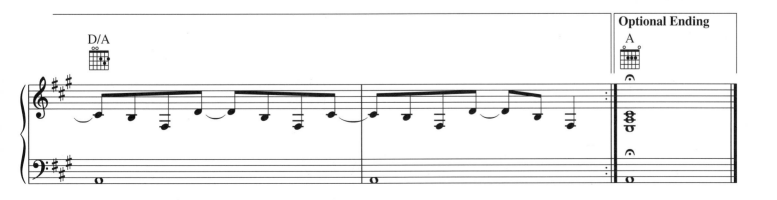

HOLES IN THE FLOOR OF HEAVEN

Words and Music by STEVE WARINER
and BILLY KIRSCH

Original key: Db major. This edition has been transposed up one half-step to be more playable.

watch - ing o - ver you ___ and ___ me. ___

Well, my

58

HUSBANDS AND WIVES

Words and Music by
ROGER MILLER

chief cause in the de - cline in the num - ber _____ of hus - bands and wives.

HOW DO I LIVE

Words and Music by
DIANE WARREN

I HOPE YOU DANCE

Words and Music by TIA SILLERS
and MARK D. SANDERS

I JUST WANT TO DANCE WITH YOU

Words and Music by ROGER COOK
and JOHN PRINE

I don't want to be the kind to
caught you look-in' at me when I

hes-i-tate ___ and be too shy, ___ way too late. ___
looked at you. ___ Yes, I did. ___ Now ain't that true? ___

I don't care what they say oth-er lov-ers do, ___ I ___
You won't get em-bar-rassed by the things I do, ___ I ___

IF YOU EVER HAVE FOREVER IN MIND

Words and Music by TROY SEALS
and VINCE GILL

IT'S YOUR LOVE

Words and Music by
STEPHONY E. SMITH

MURDER ON MUSIC ROW

Words and Music by LARRY SHELL
and LARRY CORDLE

D.S. al Coda

They

CODA

Oh, _____ the steel _____ gui - tars _____ no long - er cry _____ and you

can't hear fid - dles play ____ with drums ____ and rock ____ and roll ____

STRAWBERRY WINE

Words and Music by MATRACA BERG
and GARY HARRISON

Original key: D♭ major. This edition has been transposed up one half-step to be more playable.

PLEASE REMEMBER ME

Words and Music by RODNEY CROWELL
and WILL JENNINGS

Original key: Db major. This edition has been transposed down one half-step to be more playable.

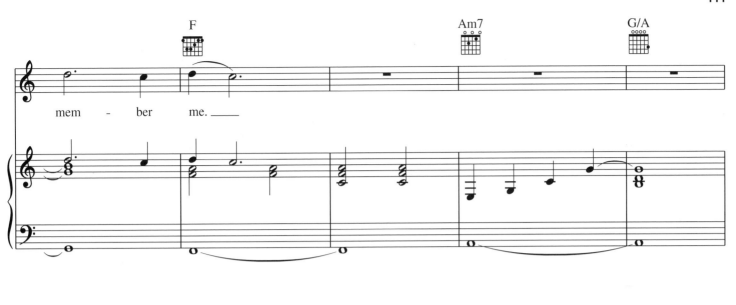

mem - ber me. ___

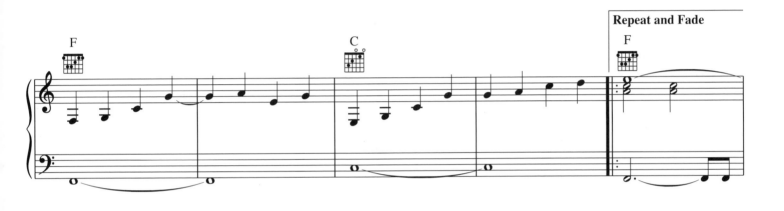

Repeat and Fade

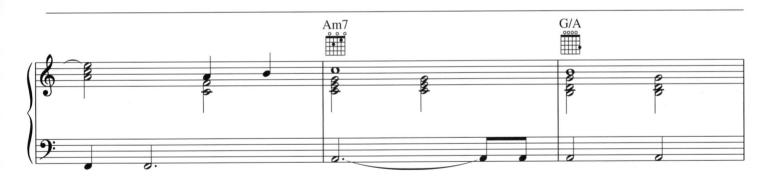

Optional Ending

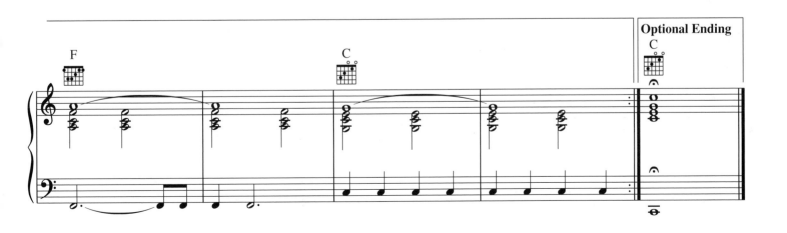

THIS KISS

Words and Music by ANNIE ROBOFF,
BETH NIELSEN CHAPMAN and ROBIN LERNER

TIME MARCHES ON

Words and Music by
BOBBY BRADDOCK

In a steady four

mf

Sis - ter cries out from her ba - by bed.
Sis - ter's us - ing rouge and clear com - plex - ion soap.
Sis - ter calls her - self "Sex - y Grand - ma."

Broth - er runs in, feath - ers on his head.
Broth - er's wear - ing beads and he smokes a lot of dope.
Broth - er's on a di - et for high cho - les - ter - ol.

Mom - ma's in her room,
Mom - ma is de - pressed,
Mom - ma's out of touch